THE EAGLE'S FLIGHT

Poems

Barry McDonald

The Eagle's Flight: Poems
©2008 by Barry McDonald

For information, address:
Sophia Perennis,
P.O. Box 151011
San Rafael, CA 94915
sophiaperennis.com

Library of Congress Cataloging-in-Publication Data

McDonald, Barry, 1952-
  The eagle's flight : poems / Barry McDonald.
    p. cm.
  ISBN 978-1-59731-091-8 (pbk. : alk. paper)
  1. Spirituality–Poetry. 2. Religious poetry, American. I. Title.
  PS3613.C38697E34 2008
  811'.6–dc22

                        2008044904

Cover and interior motifs by Lynn Pollack
Book and cover design by Susana Marín

Grateful acknowledgement is made to the editors of the following
journals in which some of these poems first appeared: *Cross Currents: The
Journal of Religion and Intellectual Life; Sacred Web: A Journal of Tradition and
Modernity; Sophia: The Journal of Traditional Studies; Sufi; Temenos Academy
Review;* and the on line-journal *Vincit Omnia Veritas.*

In Grateful Memory of Frithjof Schuon
Master of *Sophia Perennis*

"…There is one consciousness of Him, not two;
A thousand mirrors drink the single Light."

"…The liberating Word comes from the sky
Of Grace and Mercy; and we wonder why
Such gift can be; the truth is not so far:
Thy Name is That which is, and what we are."

—from *Road to the Heart* by Frithjof Schuon

for Batinah

CONTENTS

3. THE HERE BELOW

4. THE MUSIC

PREFACE

This book is a meditation on metaphysical Truth and the Remembrance of God. The poems are traditional in form and they address themes of the *Sophia Perennis*, the timeless and universal wisdom underlying the diverse religions. Lyrical and simple in style, they travel through spiritual landscapes, expressing the joy of knowing "The Infinite sings through each finite part" and "The heart's eye like a star at midnight sees." The fundamental motif of this book is the journey from conceptual understanding of the Unity of God, seen as the Absolute, the Truth or the Real, to the realization of this knowledge in the spiritual heart; "From head to heart he travels on the way." A central metaphor for this journey is "the eagle's flight".

These lines are written mostly in iambic pentameter, an ancient metrical form near to the rhythm of ordinary speech. As rhyme unifies the sonic properties of the poem, the iambic rhythm echoes the beating heart, and it is through this meter that one is drawn into the living pulse of the poem. The unity of rhyme and meter mirrors the unity of creation; the simplicity of the poems evokes the One in the many—they are like rosary beads on a single cord—and the spare quality of the poems evokes the simplicity of an invocation. And this simplicity is also a response to the Oneness of the Real, which is resistant to prolixity and cannot be divided without in some sense being falsified.

The method of composition is one of distillation; Eckhart taught "only the hand that erases writes the true thing." The poem is the child of silence and word.

The necessary purpose of poetry dedicated to *Sophia Perennis* is to transmit the perfume of Beauty; which is, according to Plato, the "splendor of the True". And its purpose is functional: without Truth and Beauty the soul lives in darkness. The final goal of any art rooted in this Eternal Religion will have as its objective the unchanging Reality of God; and it will discern the world from the vantage point of Eternity. Consequently, if song is the root of poetry, then prayer—especially understood as the deep and unwavering consciousness of the evidence of God in the nature of things —is its flower. For the person who with the open eye of the heart "sees God everywhere" through "the metaphysical transparency of phenomena"—to borrow expressions from Frithjof Schuon—God is the only Subject and the only Object, both the Seer and the Seen.

1

THE EAGLE

THE EAGLE

Because the human eye cannot see far
We pray to see things as they really are;
To rise up like an eagle soaring free,
To know and love the Truth we long to be.

And high above the valley of the soul
There is a world where time does not grow old —
No grief or laboring, no fearful night;
The dreamer wakes inside the eagle's flight.

PRAYER

Though many roads into the world appear
No matter where we turn the Lord is near.
In all the passing hours of the day
Reality is where we kneel and pray.

Men dream their lives away, but here and now
A star descends into an empty soul —
Somewhere a solitary man bows down
And with one word turns darkness into gold.

THE BRIDGE

Because there cannot be two Absolutes
The Truth is that there is no god but God.
All beauty blossoms from a sacred root
And everything we love flows from the Good.

This knowledge is a bridge to Paradise;
These words, forever new, can set us free.
Each day we rise and walk into the light
The heart knows more than what the eye can see.

THE ROAD

A man alone out walking on the road
Begins and ends his journey with a step —
This moment, passing now, he knows the Word
Of God is closer than his deepest thought.

Over his head, through broken clouds, the sun
Shines on the road and leads the traveler home.
The here below is more than just a dream —
Through every flower God wants to be known.

THE GOLDEN BEADS

The highest knowledge and the deepest love
   Cannot be separated in the One —
Both light and heat are flowing from the sun;
   Without their unity we cannot live.

Seeking the knowledge of the Absolute
   We count the rosary of stars above —
On every golden bead the Lord is proved
   And in the night we love because we love.

THE SPEAKER

Who whispers *Allah* underneath his breath?
The Speaker is more powerful than death.
The devotees to which the Word lays claim,
Their knowing and their being are the same.

Enthroned within the heart the Intellect
Is like the Sun a million stars reflect;
The people of Remembrance drink the rays,
They live inside the Name that silence prays.

THE LOOM

A unity within a Unity;
Each bird and flower forms a single strand.
The universe reflects a tapestry
And every thread is woven by God's Hand.

This carpet spreads as far as we can see —
Its weft is Peace; its warp Reality.
To know things deeply and to understand
The loom of God weaves wisdom into man.

IN TIME

—after a line by Frithjof Schuon

Lost in the ego's labyrinthine cave
Profane man is a fire, a stone, a night —
His life is a descent into the grave
And all he leaves behind dissolves in time.

But wise men see with clear, objective eyes
The worldly dream is passing, false and strange —
Day after day they practice how to die
And what they know nothing on earth can change.

VIATICUM

Discern between the Real and the unreal —
This is the most important thing in life.
Day after day the soul spins like a wheel
And what we know of life on earth is brief.

The eye of knowledge sees through many veils
  That Beauty is the splendor of the True.
  And these few words, my friend, are all in all —
  Remember God; He will remember you.

THE LANTERN

Lit by the lantern of the Name's deep glow
The pilgrims of the dawn through darkness go.
 Truth is the holy mountain they ascend —
 No other path leads to their journey's end.

And while they travel, rich in poverty,
The soul grows lighter than a summer breeze —
 And when they find the Real in ecstasy
  The heart's eye like a star at midnight sees.

AN EMPTY PAGE

Across an empty page a man may write
All of his thoughts like migratory birds;
Across the sky of silence they take flight,
In prayer they are whispered into words.

His mind grows quiet as a deer at dusk;
Becoming nothing he learns how to be.
Dressed up in dreams, the ego is a husk;
To Heaven's gate the kernel is the key.

IMMANENCE

In every age the great sages have known
God fills the world like honey in a comb.
This is the wisdom time cannot erase:
No matter where you turn there is His Face.

Until the day when you return to Him
Look for the Lord in every living thing —
Each morning when you rise invoke His Name
And know that Truth and Beauty are your wings.

THE RETURN

Although we walk together down a road
We are like raindrops falling to the sea.
The world is never what it seems to be;
The only story that does not deceive
Is telling how the soul returns to God.

Some pilgrims travel to the holy land,
While others close their eyes and sit quite still.
The reason is not hard to understand:
All of creation tends toward the Real —
Even a speck of sand becomes a pearl.

Year after year the restless soul may search —
A plain and simple flower shows the way.
Blooming out of the darkness of the earth
It turns its face toward the light to pray.

THE WISE

Among men or alone on mountaintops
The wise live in the presence of the King.
Because they see the deep nature of things
Through them a stream of prayer never stops.

Down through the centuries in every place
The saints remember God both day and night;
Some of them are like eagles in full flight
And others leave the world without a trace.

But while they live they own a single theme:
In silence and in song they hear His Name.
In different words their meaning is the same —
Because the world is more than just a dream
  Their certitude shines like the summer sun
  And they see through the many to the One.

FOR THOMAS YELLOWTAIL (1903-1993)

—Crow Medicine Man and Sun Dance Chief

So high an eagle rises in the light
It disappears, and yet it is not gone.
Its wings outspread to vanish in the sun
And there are men who sing to know its flight
Nothing lives long except the earth and sky.

Round campfires in the night the old men rest.
Their tipis softly lit; of victory
They sing with solemn voices high and free.
Each naked warrior is with glory dressed,
Brave hearts there is no better day to die.

And there are men who dance to ancient song
While others drum and dream an eagle's cry —
The mountains turn under an eagle's eye
And to that height all things on earth belong.

2

THE TREASURE

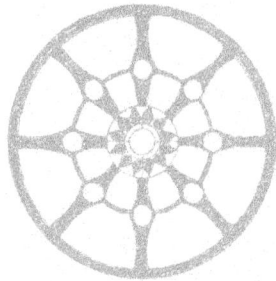

THE TREASURE

Setting a ring-stone is a jeweler's work
But sages place the Truth in every word.
Not rubies nested in the finest gold,
Their treasure is the consciousness of God.

A midnight bell rings at the end of time,
But through the darkness wisdom is revealed —
  A few wise men pass round a cup of wine
    And praise the naked beauty of the Real.

THE WHEEL

By concentration centered on the Real
The silent mind turns like a potter's wheel.
By virtue and discernment thoughts are shaped —
   Life is the kiln; Spirit in clay is baked.

Deeply awake inside a world of dreams
The potter works to fashion what he means;
   Each cup and pitcher will receive its due,
   And pour the wine and honey of the True.

THE ARK

The Orison like a seaworthy ark
Carries the only treasure we would keep.
More beautiful than any midnight star,
It is a Word that makes us pure and deep.

As we are crossing to our dying day
The core of what we know is why we pray.
Reaching the moment at the end of breath,
The man invoking God finds life in death.

LIKE SUNLIT CLOUDS

Like sunlit clouds in time we fade away;
Our fate is woven by the words we pray.
With eyes of love and knowledge we discern
The necessary things we strive to learn.

Because God lends His Oneness to the world
Remembering His Name we never part —
With souls like weather-beaten sails unfurled
Our compass needle points toward the heart.

VACARE DEO

The way of spiritual poverty
Can free a man caught in the ego's net;
The heart is made to seek Infinity
And here below it finds no place to rest.

Renouncing all but God, naked and wise,
Some men are liberated in this life —
Revealing what is beautiful and true
Their words are broken clouds the sun shines through.

THE DANCE

The timeless rhythm of our inward dance
Is measured by the click of prayer beads;
Embracing Truth in every circumstance,
Our destiny is where the Dancer leads.

Like snowflakes falling on a windy night
We travel till we reach the morning light.
Invoking God, the distance is not far —
His Kingdom is the heart of who we are.

This is the meaning of our life on earth:
Without the One what are the many worth?

THE POOR IN GOD

The poor in God are beacons of the age
And quiet words of prayer are all they own.
Through every state of soul they travel on —
The Invocation is their pilgrimage.

What is there left for them to see or do?
They find their happiness while passing through.
The ego like a wave rolls on the sea
But there is something deeper they would be:

A single voice, older than Abraham,
Weaves consciousness through flesh to say *I am.*

THE SHORE

Although men say there is no Absolute
The sun stands like a prophet in the sky.
Thinking the truth is that there is no Truth
The mind sinks root into the deepest lie.

While shadows of opinion rule the night
A few souls on the shore of morning meet;
There God still sings Himself into the light
And from the heart of silence wise men speak —

And in the moment time is flowing through
    The oldest prayer remains forever new.

THE VOW

Like rising stars that blossom in the night
The souls invoking God are steeped in light.
Their knowledge centers on one certainty:
He is with you wherever you may be.

The vow they made, taking the Master's hand,
Requires all that they are to understand
The whole they seek is found in every part:
Drinking a wine that's flowing from the heart

They touch the nakedness the Truth reveals
Till emptied of themselves they taste the Real.

THE OASIS

The true oasis in the soul's mirage,
It's there they learn what traveling is for.
The miracle of consciousness sees far
And in the heart they build a hermitage.

And as the flowers of Remembrance bloom
They wait in peace to blossom in the tomb.
What knowledge plunges them in deep delight?
What treasure buried in the ground of night?

They do not fear the fading tracks of time;
The Name of God makes earth and Heaven rhyme.

REALITY

With no vocation but Reality
The poor in God are roses on a grave;
Steeped in the consciousness of Unity
Their words are shaped by gratitude and praise.

Wrapped in their robes of silence they are free
And through the vision of the heart they see
Why should they bow to gods of lesser things?
    One song alone a naked traveler sings.

Why are they passing through the here below?
To know the Truth, and be the Truth they know.

THE RING

The vision of the heart's eye does not fail
And wise men see through the Magician's veil.
Not moving from one place they travel far,
Like stars they need not be more than they are.

Favored by Grace, abandoning all else,
Their pilgrimage leads to the deepest Self.
Like white doves flying high above the flood
All of their words are saying yes to God —

In blooms of silence where their prayers take wing
   Heaven and earth have formed a perfect ring.

SAY ALLAH

To all desires that echo in the mind,
And to the voices crying in the wind,
And to the web of whispers in our thought
We say *Allah!* Then leave them to their talk.

Because on earth we have not long to stay
We seek the hidden kingdom of the heart.
We see and we believe deep in the dark
There is a star to guide us on our way.

REMEMBER

By contemplation or heroic deed
Men find within themselves a road to God.
  The priest and warrior have little need
  And they renounce the pleasures of the world.

The body like a field in winter turns —
And like sunlight through mist, death through life burns.
  Invoke in peace, or draw swords if you must,
  Remember next to God all things are dust.

THE CHEST

A wise man seeks the jewels of the poor
But in a buried chest the gems are stored.
Within the breast is found an ancient key,
Turning the lock what does the heart's eye see?

A purifying pearl, a sacred sword,
A harp and flute to play a timeless chord;
And gazing to the very end of sight
Each ray of sun writes God into the light.

THE SAVING WORD

Morning and night we count the wooden beads;
Each is the same, strung on a single cord —
On every bead we say the saving Word
That frees us from the world and all its dreams.

Like waves that break against a distant shore
  We chant the one Word over and again —
    Our hearts bloom by the Mercy of the Lord;
    His Name has no beginning and no end.

RENUNCIATION

To rid our lives of all that is not true
In stories of desire we cannot stay.
What better work on earth for us to do —
The roads we follow are the words we pray.

The world appears like a kaleidoscope;
In changing shapes and colors men find hope.
But all that's turning one day fades from view —
    Only the Absolute is always new.

While traveling through deserts we drink wine
    Till by Eternity we mark the time.

THE MIND

The mind's an eagle meant to rise and soar,
It cannot rest until it finds the Truth:
No absolute except the Absolute —
All other knowledge, by contrast, is poor.

To see things from on high and to fly free
There is a beauty we must learn to be.
Beyond all thought of how or what or why
The eagle's outspread wings embrace the sky.

GNOSIS

The eye of certainty is like the sun —
There is no veil through which it does not see.
The center dwells in the periphery,
And as each ego thinks itself alone
All numbers must contain the number one.

The depth of God is more than we can tell;
Next to the deepest knowledge of the Real
Every religion is a heresy.
Eckhart, from whom God nothing hid, knew well:
To reach the kernel you must break the shell.

And Ibn 'Arabi, absorbed in prayer,
Saw nothing but an ocean without shore —
Its waves are flowing still through every soul:
There is no part that does not touch the whole.

THE CAVE

Although we travel to an unknown day
The Lord waits in the deep cave of the heart.
Upon the wheel of time we meet our fate
But we know God is with us from the start.

Amid a changing world God stays the same;
His Voice comes from the center of the soul.
And through the years as we are growing old
May every breath we take invoke His Name.

3

THE HERE BELOW

THE HERE BELOW

While each man seeks a candle in the night
Today few people know what life is for.
A million thoughts and feelings are no more
Than specks of dust that float in morning light.

Like birds with broken wings inside a cage
   Beyond the here below we set our gaze —
Bound from within by chains we cannot see
   The heart still beats with yearning to fly free.

THE SUNLIT SNOW

Men suffer sorrow in the here below;
There is no happiness that we can own.
The ego's burden is a heavy load
And each year chisels deeper into bone.

Through tears the mortal eye begins to see
   A man's life is as brief as sunlit snow.
The winter trees have lost all of their leaves —
   They fell to earth; to God we long to go.

KALI

The night of Kali falls over the world —
Ideas are without reason or rhyme.
In every passing year there is less time
And men forget the soul contains a pearl.

Who knows this moment is a gift of gold?
Who tells a story needing to be told?
Men think the circling wind of dreams is real
And they know nothing more than what they feel.

The stars that long ago were temple bells
Are quiet now; few men can hear them toll.
On earth there is a grief that will not heal
And in the heart grows something hard and cold —
    The age of miracles has come and gone:
    The goddess dances in the fire of dawn.

VIGIL

Men dream the shadow play of history;
  We live and die, together and alone.
The here below is not our final home;
  All men are born to face Eternity.

Why am I on the earth? And should I fear?
  Sit quietly, invoke the Name of God.
Stay vigilant, although the night draws near,
  Repeat again the liberating Word.

THE COMPASS

Still as a boulder in a flowing stream
In solitude a man sits down to pray;
A life is shaped by all this moment means
And by it he is guided through the day.

On earth there is no better work than this:
To learn what's necessary is an art —
Rooted in Being, Consciousness and Bliss
God's Name is the true compass of the heart.

SANDCASTLES

Like sandcastles beside a rising sea
There are no worldly dreams that we may keep.
Death draws us near, as waking does to sleep,
   What's nearest to the heart is all we seek.

Behind each veil discern the Absolute;
   With every lesser treasure now be done —
   With nothing but the beauty of the Truth
      The wise man will stand naked in the sun.

SANCTUARY

Closing the eyes a temple door is seen;
To enter there abandon every dream.
Where emptiness establishes its shrine,
Eternity peers through its mask of time.

Deep in the sanctuary of the mind
A bell to wake a god is all we find —
Where every moment is a prayer bead
The word that silence teaches is our creed.

THE ECHO

Invoking God, a priest of certainty
Will take the high and long view of the day;
  Because he's summoned by Reality
  From head to heart he travels on the way.

Around him every person says *I am,*
But few know where the echo first began.
  Resounding in the cave of nothingness,
    A timeless voice repeats *not this, not this.*

THE SEARCH

In search of what will make us feel complete
  We think the music of desire is sweet;
  But ego is the shell, and not the pearl —
And world is God, but God is not the world.

  A drop of water on a lotus-leaf,
  Lit by the sun this life on earth is brief.
To seek the Truth a man falls deep in thought
  But in the heart the Seeker is the Sought.

THE RADII

A man on the circumference of life,
One necessary thing he must discern:
All truth and beauty trace the radii
And from the rim to center point return.

Because he thinks so deeply of the Real
He sees God's Hand is turning *Maya's* wheel.
With each step drawing closer to the goal
Each puzzle piece is placed into the whole.

LALLA

From where her solitary dance begins
  It circles out like ripples on a pool —
Her songs like cups of wine spilled by the wind,
  Her nakedness sings like a silent pearl.

Her Master spoke to her only one word:
From without enter thou the inmost part.
  With each light step she purifies the world —
    Her soul dissolves like honey in the Lord.

THE FLUTE

A man longing to know the Absolute
Heard in a dream the call of Krishna's flute —
He followed it until, awakening,
He heard it flowing through all living things.

Its melody sings only *That Thou Art*
And each note is a flame to melt the heart.
No sleeping soul is able to resist
The smile of Krishna and the flute's sweet kiss.

THE JEWELS

A palace made of beauty will not save;
Fine furnishings won't fit into the grave.
Rich houses full of all that coin can buy,
They're prisons where the soul has gone to die.

Tending toward excess and luxury,
Without Truth beauty is idolatry.
The jewels that desire may never own,
They're purchased by our poverty alone.

What after storm and shipwreck stays alive,
The wise man knows that nothing else survives.

FLEE LUXURY

Flee luxury where kings of money rule
And culture has become the play of fools.
For those who will not take the devil's bait
Outside the castle walls the wise men wait.

With prayers sewn in everything they say
They carefully repair souls torn and frayed;
To mend the ragged world with all they do
  Beauty is thread; the needle is the True.

THE KEY

To find the narrow passage to the Lord
A man must flee the ego's mirrored hall.
In solitude he may abandon words
To find the key that will unlock his soul.

The inward way is black, but beautiful;
It leads into the deep nature of things.
And in the night when time is very still
The silent soul flies far on moonlit wings.

ORISON

A man will pray because he loves the Lord,
  Or he may know that God alone is Real;
  Soft as a breeze, or like a flashing sword,
The voice of prayer can wake the dreaming soul.

Invoking God, a man enters the heart
And finds the Knower and the Known are one.
Although clouds gather and the day grows dark
    The Invocation is the rising sun.

THE GROUND

We rise above ourselves to leave behind
The drama playing on the ego's stage;
The story of desire turns its last page
And silence fills each corner of the mind.

From that dark theater we walk away
And vanish in the heart of what we know;
Grateful to greet the full light of the day,
We stand on ground where no illusions grow.

BENARES

Today the eyes of Kali blaze,
The ego wanders in its maze;
The goddess wields her sword to cut
And by its blade the wise are taught
Regardless of the world's wild storm
They find God in each name and form.

As if the body was a cave,
A sage wrapped in a robe of flame —
In silence he has understood
God's closer than grain is to wood.

The life that he has left behind
Burns on a pyre deep in the mind —
  And in the ashes that remain
  Nothing is written but God's Name.

THE WORLD

While lovers in ecstatic moments dwell
Ascetic monks keep vigil in their cells;
A sculptor touches clay, a face appears —
A soldier prays until the Lord draws near.

Cloud palaces that drift across the sky,
Their kingdoms vanish in a traveler's eye.
A man like others who have gone before,
A page is turned and he is seen no more.

Under the witness of the rising sun
One tale, holding all history, is true:
The wisdom of the heart has always shown
From God to God the world is passing through.

4

THE MUSIC

THE MUSIC

A man who by the Absolute is touched
Is like the tone a tuning fork will sound —
The music of the soul is full and rich,
But it is false without a sacred ground.

The instruments he plays are heart and mind;
Tuned to the Truth the notes he cannot miss.
Invoking God, his practice is refined;
His song is Being, Consciousness and Bliss.

THE CHORD

A snowy mountain in a sunlit mind
And in the body like a silent sea;
In life the flowing tide of joy we find
And in the deepest heart Reality.

Since Unity sings multiplicity
A man invoking God may learn a song —
He pours himself into its melody
And hears the chord to which all things belong.

SOPHIA

She is the inward music of the Real
And when the sages sing she is their theme;
There is no melody more beautiful —
All other songs are singing in a dream.

Seeking the knowledge time cannot erase
Our journey finds an end in her embrace;
It's by her word we learn what life is worth
And by her touch, at death, the soul gives birth.

TRAVELERS

There is a sun that rises in the dark
And by its light we see all things in God.
The Infinite sings through each finite part
And by its song the captive soul is freed.

Hearing this music travelers take flight
And journey inward to an unknown height;
Deep in the silence of the heart they seek
The one established on the mountain peak.

THE LIGHT

The light sings quietly about the Lord;
It dances in the trees, turning to gold
The falling leaves that teach us how to die —
For morning turns to day, and day to night.

Because the light is clear we can see far;
Lit from within by one immortal spark
We travel long but never lose our way —
For night turns into dawn, and dawn to day.

THE HAND

Standing alone, no matter where you are,
The time and place of God is here and now.
To everyone who seeks Him here below
    He is as near as light is to a star.

The moment that is now has always been —
The center of the world is where you stand.
God's closer than the sunlight on your skin;
    He reaches out to hold you in His Hand.

THE REFUGE

A pilgrim travels on the road and sings
From God we came and to Him we return.
By what is written on the heart he learns
  His refuge is the deep nature of things.

The world around him speaks of wealth and fame;
    He listens for a moment and walks on —
All through the night the stars are stepping stones;
    The universe he lives in is God's Name.

A SINGING BIRD

It only takes a few words to praise God,
A singing bird has only a few notes.
The talk of lovers barely can be heard
Deep in the night when they are most alone.

Sometimes a single word can be enough,
A lover's glance, a moment caught in time —
The prayer a man whispers under his breath,
    It turns the water of his soul to wine.

THE TREE

The soul sinks roots into the Absolute
And by the raging wind remains unmoved;
A man whose heart lives on this consciousness
    Discerns there is no greater happiness.

Through these deep roots the sap of knowledge flows
    And through the sky a tree to Heaven grows —
        On every branch birds sing and build their nests
        And in its shade the whole creation rests.

THE GARDEN

Invoking God, we greet the break of day;
The garden that we tend is what we pray.
With love that echoes in the good we do,
We live to learn the beautiful and true.

At dawn the birds in all their voices tell
No other wisdom than the Scriptures spell.
The waking eye discerns what sages find:
Creator by creation is divined.

Eyes closed, we sow seeds of the highest art;
  What blossoms but the flower of the heart?

THE SEER

An Archetype, the Cause in its effect,
Is by the open eye of knowledge seen;
Honed by the whetstone of the Intellect
The Seer cuts the root of every dream.

And on a journey, praying in a room,
He hears an Angel singing in the tomb.
  The Limitless in every limit dwells
  And here on earth a story Heaven tells.

THE WELL

The heart is polished with the Name of God
Until the knowledge that is written there
Flows like a secret wine into the world —
Next to this knowledge nothing can compare.

As diamond is hidden inside coal,
A golden spark burns in all living things.
The soul is like a deep and holy well
And from its depth the Voice of Heaven sings.

WAYFARING

The deepest eye sees by a single star
Creation is a part of who we are.
As flowers bloom to teach us how to pray
We must be wise and watch over the day.

The beauty of the world means God is near
And on our way to Him we travel here —
The earth like an angelic mother sings;
Sunrise and sunset are her outspread wings.

THE SHELL

Because they love the Lord with all they are
Believers who have faith will go to God.
These men are made of joy and certitude
And they are long absorbed in secret prayer.

Although they go unnoticed by the world
Their words are like the sunlight and the rain.
Just as the sea inside the shell is heard,
God speaks to souls who live inside His Name.

FOR A SERVANT OF THE SELF-SUBSISTENT

How may we know what is beyond our sight?
Wholehearted prayer fills the world with light.
The further shore is infinitely near
And in the dawn of death the way is clear.

We say farewell to forms where shadows cling
And suffering is sown by seeds of time —
The soul in deepest silence learns to sing:
The Name of God alone makes all things rhyme.

THE STAR

The center of the soul is like a star;
Next to it there is nothing that is Real —
Its beauty is the light of who we are
And in creation we see God revealed.

Lit from within we travel on the way,
The one thing necessary is to pray —
As we return to God we should not fear;
   The star into the sunrise disappears.

NO DESTINATION

Like all the blessings that a lifetime brings
The snowflakes fall and purify the night.
A sandalwood stick burns, a candle sings,
A man in silence prays for love and light.

Outside a snowy path leads to the world —
There is no destination but the Name.
Because one man invokes the saving Word
There glows through darkness an eternal flame.

THE GOLDEN HOURS

The golden hours of Remembrance shine
And radiate the alchemy of Bliss;
In certitude we taste a sacred wine
And in serenity the Lovers' kiss.

Each Invocation like a drop of rain
And every star repeats the Name again;
To read the Doctrine written on the heart
We close our eyes and see deep in the dark

An Angel made of light stands in the soul;
He has outspread His wings to make us whole.

ABOUT THE AUTHOR

Barry McDonald was born in California in 1951, grew up in New England, and for more than thirty years has lived in Bloomington, Indiana. He has made a lifelong study of the non-dualist, metaphysical teachings found in the world's religions, especially in the light of the *Religio Perennis*. Pursuing this interest, he has traveled widely, in recent years making multiple trips to India and Egypt. Having completed university studies in comparative religion and literature, he was employed for many years in the business sector; he is now retired from public life. His poetry has been published in numerous journals in the United States and abroad. He has edited *Every Branch in Me: Essays on the Meaning of Man (2001), Seeing God Everywhere: Essays on Nature and the Sacred (2003),* and co-edited with Patrick Laude *Music of the Sky: An Anthology of Spiritual Poetry (2004).*

www.ingramcontent.com/pod-product-compliance
Lightning Source LLC
LaVergne TN
LVHW011409080426
835511LV00005B/456